Machines Make Fun Rides

Belle Perez

Contents

People like to go on rides.
Rides are machines.
Rides do different things,
but they are all fun.

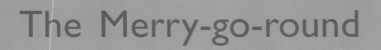

The Merry-go-round

A merry-go-round is a machine.
It has horses people can ride on.
The horses are on poles.
The poles make the horses go
up and down.

The horses are on a platform.
The platform turns around.
The merry-go-round goes around
and around.

The Ferris Wheel

A Ferris wheel is a machine.
A Ferris wheel is a big wheel.
The wheel goes around
and around.

8

9

People ride in the cars
on a Ferris wheel.
As the wheel turns, the cars
go up high.
Then the cars come back down
towards the ground.
The cars go around and around
on the Ferris wheel.

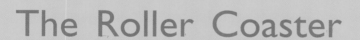

The Roller Coaster

A roller coaster is a machine.
A roller coaster has small
open cars.
The cars go on a track.

People ride in the cars.
The cars go up and down hills.
A machine pulls the cars slowly
up the hill.
The cars go down the hill
very fast.

These machines are all fun to ride.
What other machines are fun to ride?

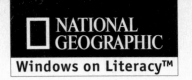

NATIONAL GEOGRAPHIC

Windows on Literacy™

Social Studies Titles • Fluent Level • Set A

Corn

From Field to Florist

Going Up the Mountain

Holidays

Ice Cream for You

Jack's Boat

Looking for a New House

Machines Make Fun Rides

Mapping North America

More Places to Visit

Our Town

Places to Visit

River Life

The Car Wash

The Key to Maps

The River's Journey

This Is My Street

Tunnels

Turn on a Faucet

Work Vehicles

Picture Credits:
Cover, 14-15, Dennis Kitchen/photolibrary.com; 1, 4-5, 6-7, back cover, Richard T. Nowitz/NGS Image Collection; 3, Gary Conner/photolibrary.com; 8, Bill Thomas/Imagen; 10-11, 16, IPL Image Group; 12-13, Chad Slattery/photolibrary.com.

Written by Belle Perez

Published by National Geographic Society, Washington, D.C. 20036

Windows on Literacy program developed by Barrie Publishing Pty Limited and Gilt Edge Publishing

ISBN: 0-7922-8932-3

Product #41031

Printed in Singapore

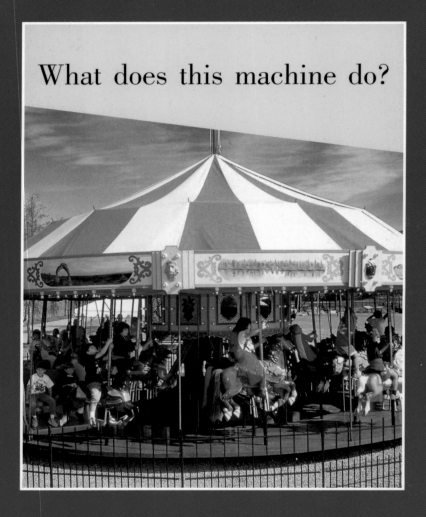

What does this machine do?

NATIONAL
GEOGRAPHIC
School Publishing

1 • • • • • • • • • • • 16 • • • • • 24

| Step Up | Emergent | Early | Fluent | Fluent Plus |

Social Studies • Set A

ISBN 0-7922-8932-3

7 27994 41031 7

Gingerbread

Eleanor Sinclair

Teaching Notes

Fluent–Level 14

Literacy Focus

Word Count and Vocabulary
- Word Count: 134 words
- High Frequency Words: *and, I, into, of, one, the, to, two, we*
- Content Words: *gingerbread, measure, half, cup, whisk, tablespoon, teaspoon, mixture, minutes*

Reinforcing Decoding Skills
- Long Vowel Sounds: *e (beat, grease, eat)*
- Word Endings: *-s (melts, adds, stirs, uses, pours)*
- Compound Words: *gingerbread, saucepan, tablespoon, teaspoon*

Comprehension/Thinking Skills
- Following steps in a process
- Using illustrations to understand text
- Matching pictures and text

Writing/Speaking and Listening
- Writing step-by-step instructions
- Sharing prior knowledge about recipes
- Discussing reasons for following directions

Math in Social Studies Focus

Content and Thinking Skills
Math
- Identifying units of measure for volume
- Explaining how to measure volume
- Identifying numbers used to measure temperature and time

Social Studies
- Understanding how a food is prepared
- Identifying kitchen tools and appliances
- Discussing how family members help each other

Building Background
Cooking requires children to apply what they know about measurement to make a product. They must understand various measures, such as *cup* and *tablespoon*, and know how to measure ingredients precisely before combining them. They must carry out steps in a process in a certain order and know the actions required to complete each step. Following a recipe allows children to build their math, critical thinking, and vocabulary skills.

For more detailed notes and assessment options, see the Teacher's Guide or use our online guide at www.ngschoolpub.org